Bluffer's Guides

CENTENNIAL PRESS

BLUFF YOUR WAY IN MARKETING

**Joseph T. Straub
Graham Harding
Paul Walton**

CENTENNIAL PRESS

ISBN 0-8220-2212-5
U.S. edition © Copyright 1989 by Centennial Press
British edition © Copyright 1987 by The Bluffer's Guides

Printed in U.S.A.
All Rights Reserved

Centennial Press, Box 82087, Lincoln, Nebraska 68501
an imprint of Cliffs Notes, Inc.

THE MARKETING CONCEPT

Marketing involves taking a simple and obvious product or service and wrapping it in a fancy package. This is a technique that all good bluffers should learn quickly because they'll practice it throughout their careers.

Bluffers should speak of the marketing concept in reverent tones because it's the core of success for any company. In down-home terms, the marketing concept says that you stand a better chance of making a bundle on a product if you figure out why somebody wants it in the first place. To marketing people, however, this marketing concept is serious stuff, indeed. It ranks right up there with the meaning of life and qualifying for a reserved spot in the executive parking lot. In fact, the marketing concept *is* the meaning of life to heavy-duty marketers, and the best bluffers should show it the same deference as lawyers show the rule of law and doctors show the Hippocratic oath. The marketing concept implies that the consumer is king, and all of the company's efforts are geared to satisfying that consumer's wants or needs.

The marketing concept should be divorced from two other outmoded business strategies that may have worked generations ago but won't cut it today.

- **The Production Concept** – Make as much as you can; somebody's sure to buy it.

3

This myopic strategy operates on the blind faith that companies can sell whatever they manufacture. It worships technology and may lead to making better mousetraps that nobody wants to buy. It worked okay in the late 1800s for the first companies that made washing machines, sewing machines, stoves, and egg beaters, but that's ancient history. Try it today with anything from lawn mowers to recliner chairs and you'll discover that it doesn't work very well now. You'll lose lots of money. And maybe your job.

- **The Sales Concept** – Send the truck out full and bring it back empty.

  This is a slightly more enlightened view of business because at least it emphasizes sales over production. A company that follows the sales concept may be either incredibly successful (if it's lucky enough to be making a product that customers happen to want) or a catastrophic failure (if nobody wants what the salespeople are being browbeaten to sell).

Well-read bluffers in marketing will recognize the pitfalls of both concepts and argue the superiority of the marketing concept (make and sell what customers want) as often as they can. You'll come across as a progressive, in-tune-with-the-times manager.

If you're in a meeting where people have lost sight of what marketing is all about, trot out an appropriate remark to remind your colleagues of the magic of being market oriented. For example:

- "Marketing is human activity directed at satisfying needs and wants through exchange processes." *P. Kotler.* Boring, but sound.

- "Marketing is disciplined demand management." Especially useful when your marketing director is more interested in your advertising than in your sales forecasts.
- "The purpose of marketing is to earn a profit by adding the maximum value at the minimum cost." *C. McIver.* Useful in negotiating with ad agencies that have just given you an outrageously high bill for their services.
- "Marketing is the intelligence service of the corporate army." *Anon.* Be careful about using this one because some people believe that "military intelligence" is a contradiction in terms.

You'll also need to prepare yourself for the cocktail party question "And what do *you* do?" More often than not, you'll have to defend yourself against charges that you use all kinds of unethical techniques to con people (including those at the party) into buying stuff they don't really need with the help of expensive advertising that they have to pay for.

You might argue that marketing is a humanistic philosophy, one that worships the wants, needs, whims, and insecurities of the consumer-kings and helps them improve their standards of living. You might, but it probably won't get you very far, especially if there are any clever lawyers, jealous accountants, pipe-puffing economics professors, or left-wing intellectuals in the crowd. They'll all go straight for your jugular vein. Wear a turtleneck shirt just to be on the safe side.

Adroit bluffers should try instead to avoid any mention of the word "marketing" in their occupation. Much safer terms are

- **Business** (innocuous and mysterious. Could mean retailing, Wall Street, corporate espionage, or a massage parlor)
- **Research** (nicely ambiguous, but don't use it if there are any academics in the room)
- **Executive** (sounds impressive; could mean anything)
- **Manufacturing** (sounds solid, but boring)

Good bluffers resist the temptation to justify the ways of the marketing world to the masses. The media's only interest in marketing is making news out of marketing's mistakes and ripoffs. You have been warned.

Marketing As Warfare

Unless you're a pacifist, treat marketing as war. It doesn't matter whether it's war against your colleagues, war against your suppliers, war against your channels of distribution, or war against your competitors. You're Rambo in a three-piece suit, and anything that moves is a threat. Sic 'em!

Military jargon fits perfectly in marketing warfare. You can propose frontal assaults, pincer movements, and guerilla attacks. You can recommend shock troops, counterintelligence, supply chains, tactical withdrawals, and chain of command. This makes things lots of fun for those who were rejected by the military but who always fantasized about kicking ass and taking names. Cheer up; you can do it in an air-conditioned office, which beats the heck out of being shot at or crawling around on your belly. The pay's better too.

Serious bluffers become students of the art of Japanese warfare. The classic text is Miyamoto Musashi's *A Book of Five Rings*. This seventeenth-century, teach-yourself strategy for samurai warriors contains all that budding international marketers need to know about making their way in the world. For example:

- "In all forms of strategy it is necessary to maintain the combat stance in everyday life and to make your everyday stance your combat stance." Especially while waiting on subway platforms in New York City.
- "In strategy it is important to see distant things as if they were close and to take a distanced view of close things." Binoculars help; use whichever end suits your purpose.
- "Suppress the enemy's useful actions but allow his useless actions." Erase the only copy of your archrival's new marketing program from the diskette she hides under her desk blotter while she's at lunch. Leave the file with her Christmas list intact.

As long as you're putting up this smoke screen, don't neglect the home front. Build a reputation for having inside information. Maneuver for position with your boss. Volunteer for assignments that will bring you maximum glory with minimum risk.

MARKETING NEUROSES

Marketing people are prone to several complexes, and good bluffers need to know what they are. In certain cases you may need to fake these maladies in order to look the part. In others, you'll have to sublimate them so you don't look like a weirdo.

Integration

"Integration" means that marketing people are obsessed with being the top gun in the boardroom. You'll encounter several folks who disagree with this view, of course. Namely, everyone who doesn't work in marketing.

Marketing trainees discover that there are many companies where marketing is neither the center of the universe nor the center of the organization chart. In fact, there are many companies in which the president's wife or the mailroom employees are more "integrated" into the organization than the marketing department is.

So what's a successful bluffer to do?

(1) Understand your corporate culture. This buzz phrase refers to the clique that really runs the company and makes the rules. It might be the marketing department, but it could just as well be finance, production, research and develop-

ment, the president's nephew, or the secretary who controls the personnel data base.

In a marketing-dominated company, for example, you should show lots of energy, be part of the solution (and never be part of the problem), show interest in customers (but not too much), and have plenty of action plans (neatly typed in three-ring binders) that you can haul out of your briefcase or fax to the appropriate manager in a heartbeat. Don't waste your time trying to sell nonmarketers on the marketing concept, however, unless you're mentally retarded, a masochist, or both.

(2) The second thing successful bluffers should do is acknowledge that what marketing is and what marketing people do are two different things. You don't have to know what marketing involves in order to work in the marketing department. For example, you might find lots of psychology majors working there already. They know what makes people tick, and that's what got their foot in the door. Bluffers take note.

If you find yourself in a company where marketing isn't integrated and your boss believes the Boston Matrix is a heavy-metal rock group, don't despair. Instead, enjoy the fun things that marketing people do, such as touring the facilities of advertising and public relations agencies or visiting several plants to see how the products are made. You can also polish your resume for your eventual defection to a company that *does* emphasize marketing over all the other functions.

Regardless of the situation, don't become too neurotic

about integrating marketing into the mainstream of the company unless the corporate culture is moving in that direction already.

Selling

Marketing is hot today, which means everybody wants to get into it. In popular usage it has come to mean selling with a college education, as in

MARKETING AREA	DONE BY
Property marketing	Real estate agents and time-share condominium hustlers
Energy conservation marketing	Solar heating and insulation companies
Financial services marketing	Banks, savings and loan associations, credit unions, and insurance companies
Relocation services	Moving and storage companies
Leisure time marketing	Travel agents

The best strategy when you meet someone who confuses your role with selling is to suggest that you're as much involved in selling as Shakespeare was in acting, or, if you're hanging out with other marketers, suggest that good marketing makes selling almost unnecessary. Another strategy is to admit you're in selling ("Yes, I'm in the business of selling ideas!"). This is how you reposition yourself as a communications consultant.

THE DIFFUSION
OF MARKETING AND
THE MARKETING
OF DIFFUSION

"Diffusion" is a term that marketing people apply to products that have become cult objects. They're ingrained in the national psyche more for their image-enhancing power than their actual performance. Examples might include Porsche sports cars, Rolex watches, Sperry Topsider boating shoes, and Mont Blanc pens.

As a marketer, you want to get your product adopted by trendsetters. Although expensive, it can eventually be a very profitable strategy. You have to spend enough money on promotion to convince people that your company's Solar Powered Digital Widget has a unique dash of panache. Its mere possession will inflate their egos, impress their friends, intimidate their enemies, and attract obscene phone calls from prominent Hollywood celebrities who can't get their attention any other way.

According to the concept of diffusion, once trend-setters start using your product, its popularity will spread from its original niche to the rank-and-file of today's status-conscious and impressionable society. And you will make money.

Successful bluffers should argue that it's possible for a product to diffuse too fast. When products do this they lose their prestige image and mystique, and consumers refuse to pay an arm and a leg for them anymore. Such may be the case with Izod shirts, Cross "writing instruments" (pens and pencils), and Gucci handbags. Once everybody starts buying a product as a badge of identity, it loses its value as a status symbol altogether. That's what happened with Scotch whiskey and Mercedes-Benz and Cadillac cars.

Another thing to remember about diffusion is that it works on a curve.

The Diffusion of Innovations

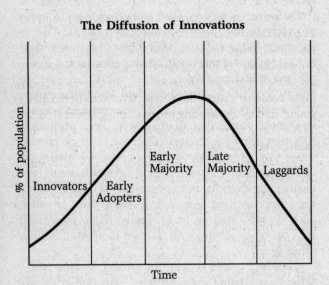

Although you may prefer to be one of the early majority (one of the crowd), you'll want others to see you as either an innovator or an early adopter—in other words, a trendsetter. Never one of the late majority or,

God forbid, a laggard. Innovators are racehorses; laggards are plowhorses. Your image is at stake.

The great thing about the diffusion curve from the bluffer's point of view is that everything, including products, people, regions of the country, attitudes, illnesses, companies, and entire industries can be plotted neatly on this curve. Take marketing itself, for example.

The innovators were American companies who adopted the marketing concept as far back as the 1950s. Procter & Gamble, one of the first, is still one of the best "blue-chip" market-oriented companies.

The early majority jumped on the bandwagon in the 1960s. These included beverage companies, which have maintained their marketing orientation fairly well, but you'd score points for astuteness if you observe during the proper strategy meeting that they're increasingly reactive rather than proactive. Retailers finally got around to discovering the marketing concept in the 1970s. They were both led and shamed into it by that master merchandiser Sam Walton of Wal-Mart.

The late majority in this parade includes financial services companies, which came thundering in in the 1980s to dazzle us with the value of their "products." (The word "product" makes a service sound less intangible and nebulous; be sure you say "product" a lot when talking about services.)

What about laggards? Well, they include politicians and publishers, who are just now waking up to the magic call of marketing. Politicians have tried to polish the confused image of their parties as well as themselves and thrown themselves headlong into direct mail promotional campaigns. Marketing research firms have been hired to position them strategically and make voters believe they can be all things to all people. If you can believe their marketing, politicians are to voters as milk is to the human body. They offer something for everyone. Yeah. Sure.

When Remington president Victor Kiam discussed the promotional budget for his book *Going For It* with his publisher, he was told that the company was going to spend $X on the book's promotion. Kiam, a seasoned business executive who appreciated the need for aggressive promotion, asked, "In which city?" The flustered publisher said that the amount quoted was the budget for the entire promotional campaign, coast-to-coast.

The route to power and success in marketing is to take the gospel of market orientation to one of the laggard businesses or industries. There are still enough of them around so that a little marketing bluff will take you a long way. Have a good trip.

SPEAKING THE LANGUAGE

Marketing, like many other professions, comes wrapped in a heavy cloak of jargon. Feel free to criticize the use of jargon, but use it for all you're worth.

Rule 1: Always refer to your company's markets in terms that are gibberish to literate outsiders.

NEVER	ALWAYS
Butter and margarine	Yellow fats
Radios, TVs, etc.	Brown goods
Washers, dryers, refrigerators, and other heavy appliances	White goods
Potatoes	White veg
Toothpaste	Dentifrices/oral hygiene
Computer programs	Software
Campers	Recreational vehicles

Rule 2: Complicate; don't simplify.

NEVER	ALWAYS
Buying motives	Composite explanatory variables
Idea	Concept
Good idea	Key concept
Bad idea	Interesting concept
Disagree or oppose	Play devil's advocate
Gradual	Evolutionary

New	Revolutionary
What we plan to do	Strategy if long-term; tactics if short-term

Rule 3: Turn obvious questions around.

For example, don't ask, "Is there a gap in the market?" Ask, "Is there a market in the gap?" Instead of asking, "What's the problem?" ask, "Where's the opportunity?"

MARKETING GURUS

Marketing, like all pseudo-professions, takes its academic gunslingers very seriously. Bluffers need to know a little about marketing's hot personalities, and it's fashionable to beachcomb for interesting bits of debris that washes up at conferences. Reveal your knowledge carefully, however, and season it with a little cynicism. Most marketing folks have a love-hate relationship with clever thinking. They love their own and hate everyone else's.

Here are a few carefully chosen gurus and some notes on their work.

Theodore Levitt

Levitt (or "Ted," if you want to impress your audience and suggest the excellence of your marketing credentials) has been connected with the *Harvard Business Review* ("HBR" in bluffers' jargon) for years. A leading professor at the school, he's probably the most able disciple of the marketing concept. A skilled bluffer should nod approvingly at the mention of two landmark Levitt texts: *Marketing Myopia* and *The Globalization of Markets*.

Marketing Myopia is required reading for all bluffers. It grew from Levitt's analysis of the decline and fall of the great American railroads. They suffered from myopia because they believed they were in the railroad business. They weren't. They were in the transportation business, and they let the airlines steal their customers right out from under them.

The principle of marketing myopia allows you to be very impressive in meetings. In a serious planning session, for example, ask your colleagues what business they're *really* in. For example, if you work in the marketing department of a bank, possible answers to the question could be

(1) Banking. (You should expect this, but the guy who says it is probably going to regret it.)

(2) Retailing. (An interesting point of view, but still myopic.)

(3) Information technology. (Make the wise guy who said this define what it really means. That should shut him up.)

(4) Dream fulfillment (by granting loans). (Encourage whoever says this to keep thinking; he or she is on the right track.)

(5) Security for people. (Aha! Whoever comes out with this one is definitely on the fast track and a threat to your job.)

Philip Kotler

Always referred to reverently as "Kotler." You should claim to have read his work at some stage of your career because his hefty textbook is considered the last word for marketing students. Guys who can bench-press it were probably starters on their college football team.

Kotler's book *Marketing Management: Analysis, Plan-*

ning and Control is sound, but reading it will put you sound asleep. It discusses such fascinating subjects as

- Demarketing
- Countermarketing
- Synchromarketing
- Remarketing

Whatever they are.

Igor Ansoff

Ansoff's is another useful name to drop, especially when you're talking about new product development. He's the author of *Corporate Strategy*, an almost-indecipherable text with one or two good pictures. Ansoff's diversification matrix is a handy way to tell the difference between existing products and new products and between existing markets and new markets. Putting the two together can provide hours of fun if you're a mental masochist.

Ansoff's Diversification Matrix

	Product	
Existing		New
Existing Market	Penetration	Product Development
New Market	Line	Diversification Extension

Michael Porter

Porter is another Harvard man who reinforces the university's dominant share of the marketing guru business. He's a specialist in analyzing competitive forces. His books *Competitive Strategy* and *Competitive Advantage* will look good on your office bookshelf. You might even have your copies autographed, if you can find a subway conductor or lobby guard whose name is also Michael Porter. Adds a nice touch of credibility.

J. H. (Hugh) Davidson

Davidson is a British guru with a blue-chip resume in marketing and a large inventory of aggressive marketing tactics. His recently republished manifesto *Offensive Marketing* is a terrific rite of passage for marketing virgins. Bluffers who are old enough should claim to have read the first edition "when it came out." That means in 1972 for hardcover or 1975 for the Penguin paperback.

Joel Garreau

Garreau, an editor at the *Washington Post*, wrote *The Nine Nations of America* in 1981. He posed the idea that North America is divided into nine "nations," and their citizens have markedly different attitudes and lifestyles that marketers should know about and take advantage of. His nations have such interesting names as Mexamerica, Ectopia, The Empty Quarter, and The Foundry.

Although Garreau may not be a card-carrying marketing guru, his book is required reading in many marketing courses and lots of consumer product companies. An accomplished bluffer should toss around the names of his nations as if everybody knows what they mean. Few people will, but you should act as if they ought to and are really out of touch with what's happening if they don't.

MARKETING TYPES

There are three basic types of marketers: the Academic, the Action Person, and the Streetwise Operator. The problem is to decide which type best suits your personality, because qualifications and knowledge are irrelevant. The important thing is to play the role convincingly. A beginning course in acting at your local junior college might help.

The Academic

Behave as if you graduated from Yale or Harvard, even if you're a high-school dropout. An awful lot of marketing people really did graduate from Yale and Harvard, however, so don't make any wild claims that you can't defend. You can say you studied history, English, modern languages, or perhaps something scientific, but steer clear of economics.

Bluffers who decide to be academics should read the *Journal of Marketing* and be conspicuous about it. Have it lying on your desk or on top of the contents of your briefcase. Keep a clip file of articles from it and several more obscure magazines on the credenza beside your desk.

You will have read Peters and Waterman's *In Search of Excellence*, of course, but make sure to mention that its sequel, *A Passion for Excellence*, is better because it's more action oriented.

Academic marketing bluffers don't do things without lots of preliminary research and feasibility studies. Nevertheless, they're quick to declare that they're action oriented. They've also read other popular business classics such as *The Peter Principle, Up the Organization,* and *Further Up the Organization.* Don't admit to reading these books, however, so you can pass off their down-to-earth wisdom as your own "concepts" or "insights."

Academic bluffers should also dress well. Herringbone jackets with leather elbow patches look nice. Bow ties add a dash of ivory-tower eccentricity that's always in vogue. Drive a BMW (which everyone will assume was paid for by lucrative consulting engagements), and admit to playing tennis or golf in college, but not recently.

Feel free to take frequent vacations, but clarify that they're not for entertainment or relaxation, but to recharge your "creative batteries." Refer to Levitt and Porter as your mentors.

Strategists are a subgroup of academic bluffers. These people share most of the behavioral traits of academic bluffers, but they're less flashy and more addicted to smoking a pipe. A pipe is a useful prop because you can't stick your foot in your mouth while you're puffing on it.

A strategist should constantly ask colleagues and superiors whether a particular action meets the organization's strategic objectives. Since there's a good chance that most people won't remember what the heck they are (let alone the corporate mission statement), you can score several attaboys with this question. All you need to remember is that the actions of people who can help you advance your career are always in line with the company's strategic objectives. The actions of the rest aren't.

You can increase the impact of your questions by citing obscure analogies from military history. "Is this the Somme in early 1916?" you might ask, "or perhaps the Sino-Manchurian conflict of 1905?" This ploy is guaranteed to leave everyone else speechless—especially history majors—and the floor will be left to you to draw your own conclusions.

Be careful of offering too many definite answers because strategy deals with long-term issues that aren't clear cut. Your military hero could be Robert E. Lee, who was short-spoken, down to earth, and intolerant of fools.

The Action Person

The action person's credo was best summarized by former CIA Director William Casey: "Set tasks. Set deadlines. Make decisions. Act. Get it done and move on."

Education and background are irrelevant. Just use a curt and heavyweight style of memo writing and delegate everything to somebody else. Action people assign tasks, set deadlines, take credit for many decisions (but only those that were correct), take credit for lots of action, then move on. This last step is especially crucial because if you stay in one job too long, the consequences of your decisions and actions might catch up with you. It's harder to hit a moving target.

Unlike academics, action people don't have the time to read lots of marketing journals. Instead, have your subordinates go through them with a Hi-Liter and mark articles for your attention. If you ever bother to look at the journals' at all, it'll just be to read the job advertisements.

If you acknowledge any business guru at all, try Peter Drucker. He was the guy who said, "Concentration is the key to economic results." Or, in the words of Peters and Waterman, "Stick to your knitting."

When you entertain, do so at trendy but newly discovered restaurants. Claim that you don't have time for vacations—except for the occasional weekend skiing in Tahoe or windsurfing in Corsica. Your heroes are entrepreneurs like Steve Jobs (Apple computers), Arthur Jones (Nautilus exercise equipment), and Sam Walton (retailing). Show respect for these people, but not *too* much.

The Streetwise Operator

This is the most difficult type of marketer for bluffers to emulate. You must have left school early—preferably after organizing some wildly profitable and slightly off-beat business that you ran from a campus telephone booth. As an alternative, you might have started in a flea market or a corner of your parents' garage. You'll credit your success to a gift for seizing opportunities that no one else recognized, and you will have climbed from rags to riches (exaggerate both) by force of your magnetic personality and a talent for turning lemons into lemonade.

Bluffers who act like streetwise operators should pay no attention to market research or marketing theory. Your instinct (be sure to call it "gut feeling") is what counts. For example, you'd much rather be out in the field selling or talking to customers than working behind a desk. This will justify your demands for a generous expense account that you spend on late night entertainment for customers.

How about your wardrobe? Well, it's mostly irrelevant, but be sure it's different from those of your colleagues, who are likely to dress in contemporary cookie-cutter style. When you finally make the big time, you'll pilot your own helicopter. Until then you drive something unusual. Like a motorcycle. Or a custom van with a mirrored ceiling.

Streetwise operators have a simple marketing philosophy: pile it high, make lots of noise, and sell it cheap. You won't care much about the product you're dealing with, but you'll threaten to cripple anybody who badmouths it. Reserve your greatest contempt for wimps of any variety. Make a point to order three-alarm chili when lunching with colleagues who've ordered quiche or gazpacho.

The early days of your career should be spent running another business on the side. This will probably make you your first million. Later on you'll have the time and energy to get into highly conspicuous consumption like Donald Trump.

Your heroes will be people like Harry Figgie and Alan Sugar. You should know and quote Sugar's remark that some companies love and care for their customers, but "at Amstrad, we want your money." You should also know that Amstrad comes from Alan Michael Sugar Trading, and Figgie International comes from . . . well, you figure it out.

So, that's the nuts and bolts of the streetwise

operator's mystique. If you do a good job of bluffing this role, you'll make lots of money for people who are sharp enough to appreciate how good you are. Including yourself.

THE MARKETING HIERARCHY

The marketing hierarchy in most organizations has several key players. They are

General Manager–Somebody who has climbed beyond marketing into the upper management stratosphere. Still likes to get involved occasionally–usually with advertising, which is safe to meddle with because it's so subjective. Anything *might* work. Treat with apparent respect.

Marketing Director–The person responsible for all marketing activities. Popular with the Postal Service because of the mountain of love letters delivered every day from advertising agencies.

Brand Manager–The person responsible for everything that happens with a particular brand. Reports to the Marketing Director. Worries about everything.

Assistant Brand Manager–The person who gets blamed by the brand manager whenever something goes wrong. An endangered species that takes Maalox intravenously before going to work in the morning. When you're right, no one remembers. When you're wrong, no one forgets.

Marketing Assistant–A marketing trainee with sales experience.

Marketing Trainee–A marketing major who just graduated from college. Knows a lot about such trivia as sales volume, customer demographics, etc. Very preoccupied with their jobs, because they haven't yet caught sight of their careers.

MARKETING AND ITS INTERFACES

Two sets of people should be considered here: those inside the company and those outside the company.

Insiders

Marketers see themselves at the center of the organizational wheel, which is natural enough. A few other colleagues (those in production, finance, and engineering, for example) may have a slightly different view.

Marketing bluffers will defend their position as the center of the corporate universe very logically. Business must meet customers' needs at a profit, which means that customers and their needs ought to be the focus of every profitable company. And guess who deals most closely with customers and needs? Right!

Support for this attitude comes from Englishman Hugh Davidson, who defined marketing as "the total approach to business which places the consumer at the center of things." Two other quotes work well too: "Markets don't pay bills; customers do," and "Customers make payday possible." This builds support for marketing's directing the sales and production departments, and accounting should be advising marketing on how to do so profitably.

Trouble is, these departments won't tend to agree. Conflict, also known as company politics, will arise.

Your conflict with the sales department will be the bitterest. This is because it's a class struggle, sort of like the running battle between liberal arts majors and MBAs. There are two ways to deal with the sales department.

(1) Be publicly aggressive but privately one of the gang. This may allow you to get away with lots of things without being mugged by a briefcase-wielding sales rep.

(2) Recommend that higher management consolidate the sales and marketing departments into a single department titled—you guessed it— marketing. The proposal may fly because you'll have less duplicated effort, a tighter organization chart, and various other benefits. Check any principles of management text under "Reorganization" for details.

Dealing with the production department isn't as much trouble. Nobody pays attention to them anyway, because today's businesses want to be market-driven instead of product-driven.

Bluffers should acknowledge, however, that quality control and on-time delivery are vital when the marketing concept hits the real world. Insist that your production people take pride in what they're making. This will win you lots of points with plant production managers, and their loyalty certainly can't hurt your career—especially when your biggest customer calls and asks you to move a delivery date up by two weeks.

Active conflict with the accounting department is dangerous. Vice presidents of finance still have lots of clout – especially in subsidiaries whose stockholders have plenty of expensive paper floating around in the stock market.

Privately, you can dismiss accountants as "bean counters" and wisecrack that "Old accountants never die – they just lose their balance." Point out how pathetically the American auto industry responded to Japanese competition in the mid-1970s as an example of what happens when accountants get their inky fingers on the levers of power.

Publicly, however, you should adopt a hard/soft approach. On one hand, try to bury accountants with reams of market research data. Computers can provide lots and lots of printouts by just punching a few keys. On the other hand, appeal to accountants' entrepreneurial instincts (if they have any). Go for the Big Idea. Even if you don't convince the accountants, you'll impress everyone else.

Finally, make sure that two groups of in-house people are always on your side:

(1) Secretaries – invaluable for last-minute word processing, setting up impossible meetings, providing information on the boss's state of mind, cutting off unwanted phone calls, booking the best hotels and restaurants, and bending the rules.
(2) Whoever has the key to the bar in the executive dining room.

Outsiders

One outside group you'll definitely have to deal with

is *advertising agencies.* The trouble with them is they always expect to be paid.

Ad agencies, like lawyers and CPAs, range in quality from good to awful, but this doesn't make a dime's worth of difference in their fees. Check it out sometime. Some agencies operate on a commission basis, which theoretically means that the agency costs you nothing. They make their money from the discounts they receive on the media space they buy for you, then charge you the same amount as their commission. If you believe that, you'll believe anything.

The important thing is to get the best available ad agency and get the most out of it. Agencies exist to satisfy your needs and wants, just as your business exists to serve those of your customers. The marketing concept knows no boundaries. You may find that your agency doesn't always do what you want, but it should always be ready to provide you with good contacts, lavish lunches, terrific entertainment, and introductions to attractive account executives of either sex. They may even be willing to hire you if you're in the job market.

A second major group of outsiders you'll have to work with is *market research firms.* Remember three things about working with them:

(1) Give them the results you expect before they begin the research, or at least before they write their final report.
(2) Insist on an executive summary at the front of the report. This should definitely say what you want them to say, no matter what's buried in the back pages.
(3) Tell them to put the bad news on their survey

somewhere around page 297. Nobody will read that far.

A third major group, *consumers,* have been studied endlessly by marketers, marketing research firms, and ad agencies. This is because they need to know what "real people" are doing, thinking, and thinking about doing. For some quick information on what's going on in the real world, read the *New York Times* and watch for news of the latest fads in California. All the weird stuff that people do usually starts there and works its way east. Probably something to do with the weather. Also read the personals column of your local newspaper and regular columns and letters to the editor in such magazines as *Playboy, Esquire,* and *American Rifleman.* Your "field research" might consist of shopping sprees in several stores along Rodeo Drive and dining in five-star restaurants. All of these are legitimate business expenses, of course, and should be fully reimbursed by your company. Good research doesn't come cheap, you know.

Qualitative or "empirical" research is always good for a few consumer anecdotes. It may help you to know, for example, that people who shop at Wal-Mart are more outgoing or have a better sense of humor than the typical Sears, Roebuck customer, or that adolescent heavy-metal rock freaks know more about the alcohol content of competing brands of beer than you ever will.

Customers, of course, aren't always final consumers. Depending on your business, they may be the retail stores that buy your stuff and resell it to Clarence Consumer. Lots of chain retailers today sell their own private or "house" brands. Not a bad idea, considering that producers who are willing to slap a private label on a national-branded product might pick up a staggeringly profitable contract from K-mart, Wal-Mart, Sears, or Penney's. They won't have to put a red cent of marketing money behind the private-branded stuff. The chains take care of that.

Whether you're dealing with final consumers or middlemen, don't believe everything you're told. Some of the most successful products in history contradicted informed opinion. For example, office-supply wholesalers had a ho-hum reaction when 3M first unveiled Post-it notes. Today, there's hardly an office in the nation that doesn't have them. Marketing specialists scoffed when Henry Peper, a chief chemist at the Paper Mate division of Gillette Company, proposed the idea of an erasable ink pen. Peper hung in there, however, and when he finally perfected the pen a decade later, it captured seven percent of the $146 million ball point pen market in less than one year.

If you're launching a new product, you can always claim that consumers are slow to catch on to something they don't already know about. Refer to the diffusion curve for backup on this. If you know in your heart (or "gut," if you're a streetwise operator) that the product is a real dog, however, do your damnedest to get promoted (or at the very least, laterally transferred) so you'll be safely out of sight and hard at work in another position when first-year losses are reported. Your successor can cover for you.

WHAT MARKETERS DO

1. Develop Market Plans

Marketers, like politicians, come in many hues and views. And just as politicians have to face elections from time to time, marketers have to get through marketing plans. Both activities are similar because they rehash the past, gloss over negatives, highlight positives, and promise what they know they can't deliver in the future.

The future is very important to marketers. This sets them apart from financial people, who often deal with the past. Superficially, a marketing plan is a bit like a balance sheet or income statement, but while these statements connect with the past, a marketing plan looks ahead.

It's easy to get excited about looking into the future – especially when it happens to be yours – but always remember that visions stretch credibility, especially with CEOs who have seen it all before. If you crawl too far out on a forecasting limb, someone – or something – is certain to saw it off.

Marketing plans come in several varieties. For example, there's a Brand Plan, which forecasts sales and profits for a specific product. There's also a Strategic Plan, which covers several years. Businesses develop company-wide strategic plans, which govern the strategic plans for all the brands they sell. There's also a Budget, which shows how much we intend to spend, how much we intend to sell, and how much profit we hope to end up with when all the dust clears. Good luck.

Plans may cover any time frame from a year to a decade or more. The longer the period, the less likely that people will take the plan seriously.

Most marketing textbooks tell you that good planning happens only when the business has been thoroughly analyzed by asking several key questions. These questions, as far as bluffers are concerned, are

OPEN QUESTION	HIDDEN QUESTION
Where are we now?	What am I doing here, anyway?
How did we get here?	Who is responsible, and why has he got a better company car?
Where do we want to be?	Where do *I* want to be?
How do we get there?	How can I get my resume typed without the boss seeing it?

Marketing plans hinge on several key concepts that every bluffer should be aware of.

Segmentation

Ted Levitt said, "If you're not thinking segments, you're not thinking marketing." It's worth remembering. Market segmentation doesn't mean dismembering your marketing director into small pieces with a chain saw — although you may be tempted to do that at times.

It means selling to a subgroup of total users with enough money to make them worth your while.

Consumers in any market have different needs that can be satisfied by either similar or identical products that are simply promoted to a particular segment of the market. How do you segment? By demographics (regular folks call them characteristics) such as

- Age
- Lifestyle
- Personality
- Marital status
- Income
- Education
- Occupation
- Average product consumption per week, month, etc.
- Buying habits (such as K-mart versus Neiman-Marcus shoppers)
- Self-image
- . . . and various combinations of these things

Segmentation is one of the easiest marketing ideas to illustrate. Take Anheuser-Busch beers, for example:

BRAND	MARKET SEGMENT
Busch	Macho, blue-collar men who worship pit bulldogs, good-lookin' wimmen, 4×4s, and beer, though not necessarily in that order. They enjoy the outdoors ("Head for Busch beer; head for the mountains.").
Budweiser	Macho, blue-collar men who just got a pay raise. Also (depending on the

	ad) college students, adults gathered around the backyard barbecue, and practically anyone else.
Michelob	Yuppies who are out for a night on the town ("The night was made for Michelob.").
Michelob Light	Weight-conscious yuppies.
Bud Light	Anyone who drinks Miller Lite. Currently endorsed by Anheuser-Busch's "senior party consultant" and party animal (who nonetheless knows when to say when) Spuds MacKenzie.
LA Beer	Socially responsible drinkers who want only half the alcohol (and, coincidentally, half the taste) of regular beer. Drink this if you can't find a designated driver. Better yet, stay home.

When it comes to segmentation, then, you're limited only by your imagination and that of your marketing research agency. Today's marketing research has developed progressively more "focused" (elaborate) segmentations of each and every market. There's a rumor that a new hiking boot now in development will be sold only to a hermit named Bob who lives in a cave somewhere in Oregon.

Segmentation is the tool to use if you want to develop a new product, maximize the sales of an existing one, or avoid cannibalization. Cannibalization, by the way, happens when one of your new brands robs sales from one of your existing brands instead of the competition. This, of course, is commercial suicide. There was speculation that Miller Genuine Draft beer grabbed a good piece of the market from Miller Lite and regular Miller instead of Anheuser-Busch's Budweiser. Pity the poor brand manager for Genuine Draft.

Two key questions should be asked about any market segment.

(1) Does this segment help us understand our customers better and sell to them more effectively?
(2) Will this segment be around for awhile (and therefore be profitable to sell to in the first place)?

The Product Life Cycle (PLC)

The PLC can be used to explain why sales are drying up. It shows which stage the product has reached between its birth (introduction) and death (decline) and what changes in advertising, personal selling, etc., should be made.

The PLC is based on the idea that the lives of products, like people, go through four phases:

(1) Introduction—High costs, low sales, and low profits.
(2) Growth—Rapidly rising sales and profits.
(3) Maturity—High sales but declining profits because competition comes in and forces prices down.
(4) Decline—Consumers shift to new and better products (such as electronic calculators instead of slide rules), or the novelty fades (as with Cabbage Patch dolls). Sales and profits dry up.

Portfolio Planning

This provides an excuse for complicated matrices. It's a powerful idea that made lots of money for the Boston Consulting Group, and adept bluffers should know all about it.

Subsidiaries or brands are plotted against the axes of market growth rate and relative market share. You end up with four quadrants, each with its complement of SBUs (Strategic Business Units):

- Stars – Fast growth and high market share
- Cash cows – Slow growth rate and high market share
- Dogs – Slow growth rate and low market share
- Problem children or question marks – Low market share but high growth rate

The question is, should you join in a portfolio planning session enthusiastically or launch an attack? If you want to join in, talk earnestly about the strategy for each SBU or brand, perhaps recommending that the company either build, hold, harvest, or divest. Use the diffusion curve to interrogate your colleagues about the product's life cycle stage.

If you want to attack, suggest that the company stick to its knitting, and criticize the principle of diversification that underlies the portfolio planning strategy. Mention Peters and Waterman's analysis of their "excellent companies," and point out that they didn't think much of diversification and the Boston Matrix. Maybe because their consulting group didn't invent it.

The Boston Group Matrix

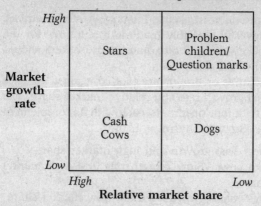

An academic or a strategist should support portfolio planning enthusiastically, but be sure to declare your belief in the power of the company brands that you're responsible for. You can afford to differ only if you're an action person or a streetwise operator. Even then, you're probably better off denying specialized knowledge and perhaps even saying things like "I know this sounds good in *theory*, but . . ."

The Emergency Matrix

There will be times when the need for a marketing plan hits your office like a thunderbolt from Zeus. It may come, for example, from an unannounced visit from the vice president and northwest regional coordinator for Montana, who loves comparing your marketing plan to that of an up-and-coming buggy whip manufacturer in Keokuk, Iowa.

Bluffers who've got to produce a marketing plan at a moment's notice have three alternatives:

(1) Repeat the last marketing plan and hope the VP doesn't notice. This is risky, to say the least.

(2) Have an outside consultant prepare a new plan. This will probably take too much time.

(3) Use this special emergency matrix for developing a marketing plan.

Strategy   Marketing mix

	Product	Price	Promotion	Place	Positioning	Packaging
innovate						
imitate						
adopt						
adapt						
ignore						
hold						
improve						
enter						
harvest						
exit						

Several key elements of a marketing plan are at the top. A list of things you can do about those elements runs down the side.

Take several transparencies of this matrix into your meeting, along with a box of multicolored overhead projector pens.

Tell the group that because planning is a continuous process, you'd like to lead a brainstorming session where each strategy is rated for effectiveness from 1 to 10 against each element at the top of the matrix. Comparisons with the Keokuk company are the subject of another transparency, of course, and should be encouraged.

After about five minutes everybody should start arguing—led by the vice president. Sit back with your spare matrix and mark it up according to the tone of the meeting. After about 45 minutes, announce that you'd like to summarize the discussion so far and examine the chosen strategies in more detail.

Present the chart and a series of agreed-upon next steps, then sit down. With some luck, you'll have saved yourself a week's work. Note: this only works once.

Marketing Economics

It's essential to be familiar with the financial jargon you'll encounter in marketing plans and budgets. The most important terms are

Sales volume—Your brand's sales in dollars or units.

Net sales—What your company actually received after sales returns and allowances.

Gross profit—Net sales minus cost of goods sold.

Net profit—Gross profit minus all expenses (utilities, insurance premiums, rent on corporate headquarters, and the annual overhaul and marina storage on the chairman's yacht).

Break-even point—The point at which revenue from sales equals total costs. Below this point, you're losing money. Above it, you're making money. The further above it you go, the more money you make.

Profit margin –The money you've made on a product, expressed either as a percent of gross sales volume or net sales volume.

2. Hire Marketing Research Firms

This, the second major thing that marketing people do, is important because marketing relies on information. You can't sell blind. (Remember what a bad idea the production concept was?)

Because marketing is consumer oriented, meeting consumers' needs has been compared to a boomerang. The return trip is a load of research data that knocks you flat after you or your marketing research firm has asked simple questions about what consumers want. So don't ask *simple* questions.

Marketing research fuels the marketing process, and like many fuels, it's expensive, damaging to the environment, and will only take you so far. This hasn't kept it from becoming one of the country's growing industries, however.

There are many kinds of marketing research, and the field is loaded with semiritualistic jargon that may baffle an unprepared bluffer. Don't let it throw you. The best strategy is to use common sense to penetrate the cloud of non-words that envelops most marketing research proposals. The basic types of market research you need to know about are these:

Quantitative

Comes from the Latin word "quanto," which means, "by how much?" This research usually involves watching and counting large samples of people, cars, planes, or whatever, and expressing the results in percentages. A typical quantitative finding might be "55 percent of all southern college students go water skiing at least 10 times per year."

Qualitative

Comes from the Latin word "qualis," which means, "of what kind, sort, or nature?" This research explores attitudes and motivation in depth. A typical finding might be "Southern college students who go water skiing do so to meet other people, not for exercise."

Quantitative researchers have historically been the underdogs who toil away in obscurity. Their reports were often important but terribly boring except to accountants or actuaries. By contrast, qualitative researchers tend to claim the limelight with sexy research techniques that involved hidden video cameras and such. They provide good stories about the lifestyles of single people in Orlando and the social mores of Yuppies.

There are two main reasons that qualitative research people tend to outshine their numerical counterparts. First, they tend to be personable, intelligent, glib, and good listeners, which means they have little trouble bluffing their way in marketing. Remember this. Whenever you hire a marketing research firm, you're buying the interpretive and marketing skills of one or two key people. If they're good, hang on to them. If not, fire them, no matter how flashy their presentations are. You'll often find an inverse relationship here. Stale, "me-too" ideas are frequently presented with high-tech support, but don't let 'em dazzle you with footwork.

The second reason that qualitative research firms seem popular is their viewpoint. Qualitative research at its best deals with tomorrow. It's thought-provoking, relevant, visionary, and hard to disprove. By contrast, quantitative research has traditionally looked backward to the number of people who did something yesterday, last month, or last year.

Quantitative research has recently started battling its drab image, however, and the major weapon in its arsenal is the microcomputer. A computer literate bluffer can score big points. Nevertheless, you don't need to know anything about computer techniques or technology, just a few useful concepts.

The best concept is the idea of *modeling,* which is building a computer model of how a particular market segment behaves. Once you've set up the model, you can ask endless "what if . . .?" questions and have the computer crank out the hypothetical results.

Another useful computer application is ultra-fine *targeting* for direct sales in person or by mail. New technology and nifty software lets you locate not only the towns and regions where market segment members live, but also their streets, subdivisions, and apartment complexes. Sort of like a surgical strike in nuclear warfare.

Continuous surveys are major studies clients buy on a regular basis in order to measure markets, retailer purchases, consumer sales, and changes in consumer attitudes. The annual cost to subscribe to one of these services may approach the GNP of a third-world country, but the information is impressive.

Retail audit presentations usually lead to a shouting match between sales and marketing. This is because one side claims the figures are too low and the other claims they're too high. Try to get a ringside seat, but don't get caught in the crossfire.

Focus groups explore consumer dynamics. Researchers round up a bunch of consumers, put them in a room, and pay them to discuss their innermost fantasies about such products as pizza, suntan lotion, and cat litter. Don't confuse focus groups with amateur photography clubs.

Tracking studies are used to intimidate ad agencies when they unveil a pathetically low unprompted awareness score for your product. (Unprompted awareness is what sorts out the real winners. It's easy for consumers to tell researchers they've heard of a name on a card, but if they reel off the names of several products without any help, those products are probably leading the pack in sales.)

Ad hoc research is done to meet specific objectives on a marketing problem not covered in continuous surveys. Ad hoc research can be quantitative or qualitative, upscale or bargain basement. When you think about hiring a firm to do an ad hoc survey, remember this rule about marketing research: "The usefulness of any research is measured by the ability of those on the receiving end to do something practical with it."

Marketing research has revealed lots of fascinating facts. For example, the *Wall Street Journal* reports

- Most people prefer a blue toothbrush.
- Forty-seven percent of people put water on a toothbrush before they apply paste; 15 percent after; 24 percent before and after; and 14 percent don't wet it at all.

- Americans take 52 million aspirin and 30 million sleeping pills each year.
- The average person blows his or her nose 256 times a year.
- Ninety-one percent of Utah residents pump their own gas, but only 33 percent of Maine residents do.

Market Research Jargon

ABC (Audit Bureau of Circulations) –The last word on newspaper and magazine circulation. The wider the circulation, the higher the cost for advertising space.

ACORN (A Classification of Residential Neighborhoods) –Who lives where.

TGI (Target Group Index) –A survey popular with the media to demonstrate that their magazine is read by more bleu cheese dressing users than anyone else.

TAT (Thematic Apperception Test) –Getting consumers to describe their feelings with crayons and pieces of paper.

CATI (Computer-Assisted Telephone Interviewing) –Work that allows unemployed actors to practice their interpersonal skills with the help of the Manhattan telephone directory.

UPC (Uniform Product Code) –A unique pattern of lines of different widths that identifies a product's brand, size, etc. Supermarket computer scanners read the UPC and automatically ring up the product's price. Found on just about everything today. Rumor has it that federal law will soon require newborn children to have their name, sex, address, and other personal data tattooed on a bar code on their foreheads. This will make it easier for the Internal Revenue Service and Social Security Administration to stick their noses into our business.

SAMI (Selling Areas Marketing Inc.)—A research subsidiary of Time Inc. that collects sales data from more than 100,000 food stores nationwide and reports on what's selling best and where. According to *Fortune,* SAMI claims that Indianapolis is the leading national market for shoe polish, Miami for prune juice, Grand Rapids for rat poison, Denver for vitamins, and Salt Lake City for candy bars and marshmallows. If you can't afford to subscribe to its services, ask a sample of any ten women at the nearest supermarket. They'll probably give you the same information, only cheaper.

STM (Simulated Test Market)—A fashionable method of testing the success of your marketing mix.

DAR (Day After Recall)—Advertising testing technique on which to pour scorn, unless you work for Procter & Gamble.

ECG (Extended Creativity Group)—A bunch of consumers, TATs, beer, and snacks all thrown together in one apartment complex recreation room for an afternoon.

ABC1C2DE—Social grades. Also known as SEGs (Socio-Economic Groupings. A's are judges and generals, B's are marketing people, C1's are IRS auditors, C2's are heating and air-conditioning repairmen, D's are garbage collectors, and E's are elderly parents and irresponsible college kids.

OTS (Opportunities to See) –The average number of times the target audience is supposed to see your ad.

ADT (Afternoon Drive Time) –A time period during which most commuters are imprisoned in their cars making silent (and not-so-silent) single-digit gestures at each other while wending their way home on the interstate at 80 miles an hour. This, along with MDT (Morning Drive Time), is supposed to be an excellent time to run a radio ad. Especially for assault rifles.

3. Launch New Products

Marketing people must also launch new products because these are a company's lifeblood. What's less obvious is that marketers often spill somebody's blood (including their own) to make these new products successful.

Only one in 20 new products succeeds. This means that only one in 20 new product *managers* succeeds, so successful bluffers should look out for themselves first. The products they're in charge of are secondary, but nonetheless important, to their survival. Here are several suggestions for developing your career through new products.

Ideas are not the problem.

Getting ideas is not a problem today. You'll find all kinds of ideas at trade shows, during the essential year-ly trips to Japan, or just by looking at your competitors' catalogs. You can even take pleasant field trips to your market research firm to brainstorm new ideas.

The problem you have to deal with is not ideas but the *right* ideas. In the 1970s, for example, many companies charged headlong into instant snack foods. Huge investments in plants and technology followed, the market proved to be a can of worms, and the inevitable shakeout occurred. Home computers and game software were a similar story.

As a general rule, then, don't get carried away with fads. If you don't have a piece of the action by the time they're picked up by the press, it's too late.

Know what your company's really good at.

Few companies can change their characteristics overnight. You'll stand a better chance of picking a winning product if you know where your firm's competitive advantage lies. For example, if you work for a company that makes canned and bottled soft drinks, be careful about suggesting that it get into stereo systems, satellite communications equipment, or climate-controlled support hose.

If your general manager wants to diversify into some exotic product netherworld, you might mention the importance of the "experience curve barrier." Simply stated, if your company doesn't make and market the gizmo already, you'll probably lose your shirt. This sounds transparently obvious, but it's surprising how many companies learn the lesson the hard way.

Get a product champion.

Academic research confirms the importance of a product champion to new product success. This excludes your spouse, parents, or the account executive at your company's ad agency.

The best product champion is a senior executive who believes the thing will work and will help you cut through politics and get approval from the powers that be.

The Sony Walkman personal portable stereo evolved somewhat like this. According to the *Wall Street Journal*, Masaru Ibuka, Sony's honorary chairman, walked into the office of chairman Akio Morita lugging a portable stereo tape player and wearing a pair of clumsy headphones. He explained that he liked to listen to music without disturbing others, but the headphones were too heavy. Morita directed his staff to build a pocket-sized experimental tape player with ultralight headphones, then asked the manufacturing and sales people what they thought of its commercial value. They said it was a loser. Morita ramrodded the product to market by taking personal responsibility for it and managing the project himself. He was, in effect, his own champion. The fact that he was the chairman didn't hurt either, of course.

Don't underestimate the workload.

Launching a new product takes lots of time. Everybody in the company has to be educated about it. Given the lead-time required for capital expenditures, plant expansion, market testing, package design, and ad campaigns, it's sensible to have lots of help available. If you don't have it in-house, use outside advertising and PR agencies.

Decide on a clear role for market research.

Full-scale product development calls for various kinds of market research, such as

- Early "exploratory" qualitative research
- Concept research with focus groups
- Home placement surveys
- Advertising development research
- Package design research
- Test marketing in STMs (simulated test markets)

Before you hire research firms and spend your company's money, decide what you want to do. Do you want to

- Blow the competition out of the water?
- Get the product to market come hell or high water?
- Market the product regionally and let consumer response dictate whether to kill it, keep it, or expand it nationwide?

Sell the product to your sales force.

Sometimes the biggest obstacle to any new product's success is the support of sales reps. Witness Sony's experience mentioned earlier. If they don't like it, they won't try very hard to sell it, so . . . well, you get the picture.

Gathering sales force support can be a special hassle because of role reversal. Think about it. Sales reps spend most of their time being nice to buyers who aren't nice to them. Now here you are, trying to sell *them* something. They're in the driver's seat for a change, so they'll probably make you sweat.

Don't put your faith in computer graphics and pretty

slides. Put yourself in the sales reps' shoes. It's a rainy Monday morning and you're sitting in a lobby with 27 other sales reps drinking coffee that tastes like battery acid and being held at bay by a receptionist who looks like Pee-Wee Herman and acts like Hulk Hogan. Now, Bunky, what are the *real* benefits of this product?

Watch the first few days of the product launch carefully.

If television pollsters can predict the winner of a presidential election from the first few states, you ought to be able to decide whether this project should be your responsibility or someone else's from

- The ooh-aahs (or lack of them) from middlemen at the first trade show presentations
- Consumer purchasing rates and repeat sales from test markets and ad hoc surveys

Research after the launch can be useful, but there's a delicate balance between saving your own hide and finding out how you can do better next time.

Note: Although lots of people claim responsibility for a successful product, you'll rarely meet somebody who admits to have launched a failure. Lee Iacocca said so many people claimed to be the father of the Mustang that he'd hate to be seen in public with the mother.

Avoid the consequences of failure by

- Denying the failure entirely. ("Look, guys, we got a 75 percent market share in East Armpit, New Hampshire! Now, is that good or what?")
- Blaming Manufacturing or Sales for unspecified mistakes.

- Blaming retailers for bringing out their private brand six weeks after your national brand was launched. Always a good argument – especially if it's true.
- Blaming the company for not spending enough on promotion.
- Philosophizing about the problems and costs of creating a really drop-dead product in today's competitive environment.
- Affirming the importance of taking big risks for big rewards. ("You have to break some eggs to make an omelet." "No guts, no glory.")
- Stressing the problems connected with genuine innovations. The implication is that you had the courage to think big and bet big. Just be glad the betting was with company bucks and not your own.
- Citing other new product disasters (the IBM PC*jr*, Ford's Edsel, RCA's SelectaVision, Bic's pantyhose).
- Finding another job before top management declares the product a catastrophe and has you escorted from the building at gunpoint.

New Product Jargon

Added value – What most new products claim to have. This is a generic claim used by most sales reps. It's a good excuse for a higher price.

Blind test – A consumer test without identifying the brand of product. The "Pepsi Challenge" was a takeoff on this.

Brand extension – Making the most of an accepted brand by putting it on a new product. For example, you may have noticed Ivory shampoo, Mr. Coffee coffee, Whitman's Sampler ice cream flavors, Minute Maid orange soda, and Hershey chocolate milk. Some flops or near flops: Life Savers gum and Johnson & Johnson baby aspirin. Be careful not to extend a brand too far.

Concept/product fit – Getting it right. Harder than it looks.

Insulation – Throwing up barriers against competitors who try to muscle in on the market you've targeted with your new product.

Me-too product – A competitive entry in the market that you've developed. Jumps in after your company spent millions to break the ice.

Me-too late – What you'd better not be if you decide to launch a me-too product.

No go – Try again.

Rollout – Launching a product in a succession of geographic areas instead of going nationwide all at once.

4. Brand Products

Marketers have to brand their products, because brands make one company's product stand out from the rest.

Branding is serious business. A brand name communicates such things as quality, reliability, status, distinction, sophistication, and countless other messages that impress consumers.

There's lots of difference between a product and a

brand; between cat food and 9 Lives, denim jeans and Levi's, a personal computer and an IBM PC-XT. Brands give a product an identity and implied characteristics that both the company and consumers value highly.

Another reason marketers take branding seriously is because it tends to ensure the security of future profits. It creates a pattern of loyalty (sometimes bordering on fanaticism) that converts a company's product into a profit-making juggernaut.

Branding brings other benefits, too. Having created a distinctive image with consumers, brands can be extended within their area of credibility (see "Brand extension" under New Product Jargon). Such is the case with Bic, which started out making disposable pens, then advanced to disposable lighters and razors and now even disposable perfume. (Does it smell like lighter fluid?)

Brands that are extended beyond their perceived limits or lose their value because of promotional overkill or price decreases leave themselves open to attack from competitors' brands and chain retailers' private brands. Bluffers should treat the threat of private brands carefully. Most big chains tend to offer at least a few products under their names today, and the trend is definitely established.

Positioning

If a brand name communicates the physical and psychological attributes of a product, positioning gives the brand a definite distinction in consumers' minds and in relation to competing brands. For example, Agree shampoo fights the "greasies"; Check-Up toothpaste attacks plaque; LA beer has less alcohol.

Good bluffers have to be savvy when they're positioning a brand. For example, if you're trying to position a financial institution such as The Next-to-last National Bank, you might adopt a slogan such as

- The Bank That Listens
- The Action Bank
- The Thoroughbred Bank
- The Bank That Likes to Say Yes

Although banks offer the same basic services, their positioning conveys distinct styles of doing business that are meant to appeal to a broad market segment of consumers.

Products can be positioned differently in different markets. They can even be repositioned as markets evolve or change. For example, few people remember that Marlboro cigarettes were once sold to women and had a red tip to mask lipstick smears. The company revamped the brand's image and repositioned it as a man's cigarette several generations ago.

Most marketers will run into positioning issues sooner or later, so here's a checklist to get you off to an impressive start. Simply evaluate the relevance of each word as a platform for your brand.

PRESTIGE, FUN, HEALTH, EXCITEMENT, MYSTERY, ROMANCE, STYLE, SOPHISTICATION, CONVENIENCE, QUALITY, FASHION, TRADITION, BARGAIN, FAMILY, INDIVIDUAL, CONTEMPORARY

Beware of meaningless positioning slogans. "Tomorrow's finest food today," for example, says nothing. Many words have been so ground up in today's marketing mill that they've all but lost their power and meaning.

5. Make Presentations

Marketing people must make presentations, and whatever their personal style, all successful presenters are consummate bluffers. In fact, the entire art of making a good presentation is a bluff. Successful movie actors often confirm this, but not until after they've collected their Oscars.

The content of your presentation is the least important part. It's not what you say but how you say it that counts. Go for short, pithy generalizations—a few words for each slide or chart. Intersperse these with heavyweight charts of numbers which you can pass over arrogantly as an *example* of the work that *you* have done. Then turn quickly to the three-bullet-point summary. Consider giving your audience a back-up fact sheet. They'll carry it away unread and file it for reassurance after the meeting.

Spend most of your energy on taking command of your audience. David Ogilvy always recommended reading every word on a chart exactly as it was written. He believed, probably correctly, that most of the audience wasn't awake enough to cope with two different messages simultaneously. You flatter your audience, however, by crediting them with being able to read and listen at the same time. They can't, but it should help to confuse them.

Insist on rehearsing your presentation with all the materials and equipment that you'll use. Otherwise Murphy's Law will strike you dead. This is crucial. There's no point in putting yourself in situations where you have to bluff to stay alive.

6. Buy Advertising

Marketing bluffers will also have to deal with ad agencies, which means they'll have to juggle lots of interesting responsibilities and meet lots of different people.

Ad Agency Personnel

Receptionist–The most powerful person in the agency. Probably knows more about your account than the account director.

Chairman–Interesting crossbreed of grade school principal and James Bond.

General Manager–The boss of the agency. Usually attends meetings when the agency has something to gain or lose. Asking for his opinion of the latest Nielsen ratings should shut him up.

Creative Director–High salary, high profile, and high style. Usually into Zen, Lamborghini sports cars, hang gliding, and his third wife.

Account Director–Living proof that opposites attract. Probably a defrocked marketer. Treat with a mixture of suspicion and sympathy.

Account Planner–Smart-ass account manager who turns your product's features into baby talk for the creative department. Watch out when he feels a matrix coming on.

Account Manager–Usually a nice person who gets stepped on by everyone else. Still, this is advertising, and it *is* your money you're spending.

Creative Teams – Groups that create and do so frequently, but not necessarily with advertisements. Watch them turn your product into an award-winner. A Clio award, that is. For their agency.

Media Planners – Second-class citizens in the agency who compensate for their status by engrossing themselves in frequency schedules and response functions. The nicest people to have a drink with. They might invite you to places like the Bahamas for conferences about profound subjects like "The Future of Television."

Media Buyers – People who buy time or space from TV, radio, magazines, newspapers, and other media and play a suicidal blend of poker and chess. They can save or lose you a lot of money. Don't be fooled by their capacity to drink beer.

Pitching Etiquette

One of the most curious rituals of advertising is the elaborate courtship behavior that develops between you, a potential client, and the ad agencies that want your business.

As an advanced bluffer, you'll realize the necessity to observe certain customs and practices when you ask an agency to present its credentials. (The word comes from the Latin "credo," meaning "I believe." Cynics might say that "incredentials" is a more accurate description.)

Several points of tact should be observed when you listen to an ad agency's pitch for your business.

(1) Don't laugh spontaneously and out loud as the agency discusses its philosophy or admits it doesn't have one. Agencies that have one take it

seriously and have probably spent hours of time (which clients may be billed for) developing such classics as "We prefer to work as partners with our clients" or "We offer a total communications solution."

(2) Show neutral body language during the presentation. Don't reveal interest or boredom. Jot an occasional note on the agency's pad with the agency's pen—perhaps your list of things to do tomorrow. Be sure to take the pad with you when you leave so the agency people will go nuts wondering what you wrote.

(3) When they've finished the case histories of previous successful campaigns, be noncommittal. Just say, "Thank you," and ask them a heavy-duty marketing question like "How many reserved parking spaces do you have for clients?"

(4) Then ask them a vaguely relevant question like "Do you think your campaign can help our brand recapture 20 percent of the private label market from K-mart and Sears?" After about 20 minutes of brainstorming by the agency people, say, "Thank you. That was useful."

(5) Close the meeting by asking to meet the people who would actually work on your account; then pick up whatever goodies are left lying around the conference room and leave. Remember, this is your greatest moment of power. It's all downhill from here.

High Noon at the Agency

Once you've finished playing this ritual mating game,

you have to get down to the basic problem: getting the work out of the agency. This won't be as easy as it sounds. You can be sure that at least one of the following will happen:

(1) The campaign that your company's general manager liked bombed in research, and there are just six weeks left before the sales conference and twelve weeks before the product's nationwide launch.

(2) The agency's presentation omitted a section dealing with lead time for commercials.

(3) You will receive a document from the agency's account planner titled, "Preliminary Thoughts on an Approach to the Creative Brief."

None of this is very reassuring. Shock tactics will be necessary. Arrange a meeting between you, your general manager, and the agency's general manager. Scare the hell out of the agency by threatening to

- Reject the agency's contract
- Disapprove the media expenditures
- Use an oddball creative team that currently works out of a Winnebago camper to develop the campaign
- Get an independent to buy your media at a reduced commission rate

This will get the agency off the dime. The next problem will be interpreting the jargon it uses when it presents the campaign to you.

Breaking Agency Codes

WHAT THEY SAY	WHAT THEY MEAN
Strategically sound	Boring
Well grounded	Very boring
A simple idea	Intensely boring
Featuring the product as a hero is passé	We think the product's crap
We think Mr./Ms. X (a famous celebrity endorser) says a lot about the brand	We *know* the product's crap
It blew their minds in research	Consumers think the product's crap
The product's very distinctive	It's ridiculous
The product's highly campaignable	We can make even more money than we thought
It'll work in the press	They can't afford television
It's ideal for television	There's a big budget here
Make two for the price of one	Make one for the price of two
Look how well we built on your existing property	But we had to demolish it first
Imagine the trade ad	We hope you can; we can't
The agency's view is . . .	We don't agree

7. Promote Sales

Marketers also get involved with sales promotion, often by hiring a sales promotion agency.

Good sales promotion agencies can make your money work very hard. They're more effective at getting consumers to try a product, generating sales, and creating product loyalty than any other agencies you might use.

Your original ideas are helpful here, as long as they don't land you in court for breaking one of the many laws that apply to sales promotion in general. Good ideas, both old and new, are probably a better bet. They cost little, are easy to manage, keep retailers' cash registers humming, and meet your objectives. Nobody ever won national recognition through innovative sales promotion anyway.

Be clear in your own mind what you want to do. As far as consumers are concerned, you may want to

- Get them to try it
- Buy yours instead of competitors'
- Switch to a larger package
- Reward repeat users

As far as retailers are concerned, your major objectives are to

- Get more stock onto their shelves
- Blitz your competition
- Get shelf space (at least on a trial basis)
- Raise employee awareness of your product

Finally, there are the million and one incentive schemes to fire up your sales force.

Sales promotions are about noise—creating it and

cutting through it. Remember the Hawthorne Effect: it doesn't matter what you do as long as you keep changing things. This maxim comes from a series of experiments at Western Electric's Hawthorne plant in Cicero, Illinois, between 1927 and 1932 by Professor Elton Mayo. Mayo discovered that brighter lighting, longer rest breaks, and free food increased employee productivity. He also discovered that dimmer lighting, shorter rest breaks, and no free food increased productivity. The changes were what mattered. They made employees feel important. The same idea carries over to sales promotion efforts with consumers or retailers.

Promotion Jargon

Banded offers—Attaching a new product to an established one and selling the two as a unit. The promotional equivalent of a blind date.

BOGOF—Not necessarily a curt dismissal: Buy One, Get One Free.

Contests—The lifeblood of sales promotion. Make sure to have a contest-building company write the rules and statistically debug your contest. If there are any mistakes or oversights, you can bet on a class-action suit from disgruntled losers.

Extra product—Offering a larger package with more product and a blurb such as "33 percent *free!*" Appeals only to imbeciles. The stuff's not really free; they have to pay for it.

Collaborative cross-product offers—Two manufacturers in bed together.

Price reductions—Short-term sales boost at the expense of your brand's personality and image. When's the last time you saw Jack Daniel's, Rolex watches, or Jaguars pitched this way?

POP displays – Point-of-purchase displays that decorate the store at your expense. Meant to slow down customers so they buy on impulse, which reduces your need for sales clerks. Many clerks have less personality than a cardboard cutout anyway. If retailers let producers and wholesalers set up every POP display they want to, there'd be no room in the place for merchandise.

8. Exploit PR

Like sales promotion agencies, PR agencies can be divided into those with good ideas and those with none at all. Good PR costs very little; bad PR can cost a fortune. The trick is to pick the right agency.

PR agencies come in several shapes and sizes. Those who boast about their "strategic" thinking often want to explain your own marketing plan to you. Those who offer a "total communications solution" want to do your advertising too.

To get the most out of a PR agency, you should

(1) Make sure the agency puts both a dreamer and a doer on your team. Lots of agencies bubble over with bright ideas but can't deliver on time, to specifications, or within the budget. Others can deal with the mechanics but cannot write and have no imagination and contacts.

(2) Ask for proof of the proposed campaign's effectiveness. PR agencies have worked so long and

hard to convince a skeptical public of their ability to produce measurable results that they can't refuse you this request. Whether you allow yourself to be persuaded is up to you.

(3) Get the agency to define and target each market segment you're interested in. If you want to reach the managers of major pension funds, for example, an ad in the *National Enquirer* may not do you much good.

(4) Make sure the agency does all it can to get someone else to pay for your company's PR. A trade association might kick in a few bucks for your campaign on home security systems; a major white wine or cheese producer might agree to pitch your new book, *A Yuppie's Guide to Famous Singles Bars.*

9. Call in Consultants

The last thing that marketing people do is call in consultants. There are consultants who deal with virtually any problem, and marketing is no exception.

The Ad Agency as Consultant

In recent years ad agencies have declared themselves to be experts in all areas of marketing. There are two problems with this:

(1) The traditional commission structure of ad agencies is incompatible with the largely fee-based approach of consultants. To maintain their usual levels of profitability, ad agencies have to charge

high fees in relation to the consulting services they provide.

(2) Ad agencies have only one solution to most business problems: do more advertising. This is often neither appropriate nor financially feasible.

The Heavy Hitters

Gigantic management consulting firms such as the Boston Consulting Group and McKinsey and Company will tackle marketing problems, of course. Apart from the clout that their recommendations carry, there are three things to note:

(1) You may be advised to reorganize your company from roof to cellar.

(2) International consulting firms tend to relocate employees whenever the wind changes, which means that you may never deal with the same consultant twice.

(3) The work is usually done by bright, newly minted MBAs with no experience in the real (your) world.

If you employ a heavy hitter to unravel your marketing problems, be sure you've got plenty of money.

The Rest

There's a whole grab-bag of companies and individuals who claim to be consultants. Check the yellow pages of the telephone book sometime. A consultant, as everyone knows by now, is anyone who's 50 miles from home and carries a briefcase.

No matter whom you hire, you should expect service beyond the call of duty, creativity under fire, an ability to meet deadlines come hell or high water, and the ability to think critically and intelligently. Many people believe that the last quality is least important.

You usually have to rely on past experience, contacts, and personal recommendations to pick a good freelance consultant. Be careful not to pick one with too few clients or one with too many. Remember that you're buying the skills of one or more individuals, so make sure you know who will actually do *your* work. They, too, may be bluffing.

JARGON

Jargon and marketing are inseparable, and a little jargon will take you a long way. We've presented some jargon peculiar to specialized marketing subjects earlier in the book, but this section deals with the most universal marketing jargon. Read on.

Above the line – What marketers are begged to spend by their ad agency. May make the difference between a successful ad and a Clio award-winner. The agency gets the award, of course.

Achilles heel – The company's or product's weakness.

Below the line – What everyone except your ad agency wants you to spend on advertising your brands.

Brainstorming – Generating ideas in a totally unstructured and uninhibited environment. Can be seen in most bars when happy hour winds down and the customers are wound tight.

Bundling – A Scandinavian custom of wrapping horny adolescents of the opposite sex in blankets – both around and *between* them. Raises desire and hinders performance. Marketing people do the same thing when they put two products together to convince gullible consumers that they're getting a better deal. In Scandinavian bundling, no one gets screwed. In marketing bundling, the consumer often does.

Cannibalization – Raising sales of one of your company's brands by stealing market share from another of your brands instead of from the competition.

Culture—Trendy term to explain how things are done in a company. Often used as a reason something can't be done, as in "It's not part of our corporate culture."

Cutting edge—A good thing to have in a marketing plan. Make sure you turn it toward your competition instead of yourself.

Demarketing—What marketers do to appear socially responsible. Sales of the demarketed product decrease, which means the prices of the company's other products will probably be raised to make up the difference. Has been done with alcoholic beverages (to discourage drunk driving), salt (to lower blood pressure), and gasoline (to make oil deposits last longer).

Diversification—The most effective way to boost top executives' egos and lose stockholders' money.

Economies of scale—Justification for strategic planning that calls for lots of new things such as plants, offices, warehouses, equipment, and employees. The idea is that the bigger you are, the cheaper you can manufacture something.

Elasticity of demand—What you hope exists before you drop the price. If you're right, the increased sales volume will more than compensate for the lower profit per unit. If you're wrong, update your resume.

Four P's—The ingredients in the marketing mix: product, price, place, and promotion. You can't ignore them. Don't even try.

Gap analysis – What you do to spot gaps (also known as "windows of opportunity") in the market.

Grow, harvest, and exit – The only business strategies you need. Growth is good for headlines in the marketing press and getting your next job. Harvest is good for nothing except funding growth. Exit is good for headlines, too. After you've landed your next job.

Key success factors – The keys to fame and fortune in any given market. Always ask somebody else before they ask you.

KVI – Known value item. Change the price with care, because consumers won't be easy to fool.

Line extension – The knee-jerk response to new product development assignments. Just beware of making so many varieties of the basic product that you destroy its image and cannibalize your own sales. Can be done by adding lemon, enzymes, a selection of fragrances, several new flavors, a digital readout, or a different dispenser.

Marketing mix – What happens when brand managers put the four P's together and shake them up. The best mix looks good (at least on paper), tastes good, costs a lot, and does a lot of damage. To your competition, you hope.

Matrix – The Lego blocks of marketing thought. Don't confuse with Dot Matrix. Whoever she is.

Parameter–The limit, as in "Our budget parameters don't go that far."

Projective techniques–What market researchers sometimes apply to a survey. Silly answers to silly questions at horrendous prices.

Scenario–The mess you're in or might be in if things don't change fast. A good word to use when you have to break bad news to your boss: "We're currently in a high-risk scenario."

Spontaneous awareness–What your boss never shows when you come up with a good idea.

SWOT–Strengths, weakness, opportunities, and threats. Analyzed a lot in developing marketing plans. Also known as sweat analysis for obvious reasons.

Synectics–Trendy word for brainstorming.

Synergy–A condition that exists when the whole exceeds the sum of its parts. You hope your marketing plan has it. You hope your competitors' marketing plans don't.

Test marketing–An expensive and public way to demonstrate how well you've organized a new product launch.

The three R's–A product manager's life cycle: repackage, relaunch, and resign.

Get Bluffer's Guides at your bookstore or use this order form to send for the copies you want. Send it with your check or money order to:

Centennial Press
Box 82087
Lincoln, NE 68501

Title	Quantity	$3.95 Each
Total Enclosed		

Name_____

Address_____

City _____

State_____ Zip_____